Between 1932 and 1933, about 3.9 million Ukrainians were starved to death.

This was not a natural disaster.

The United Kingdom parliament recognised the Holodomor as a genocide in May 2023.

A total of 32 countries have now recognised the Holodomor as a genocide.[1]

The Holodomor is one of the most horrific crimes in human history. The enormous number of deaths and the gruesome manner of these deaths – slow starvation – defy the imagination.

People with swollen legs, covered in sores, could not sit. When such a person sat down, the skin broke, liquid began to run down their legs, the smell was awful, and they felt unbearable pain. Children developed swollen bellies and heads that seemed too heavy for their necks. One woman remembered a girl who was so emaciated that 'one could see how her heart was beating beneath the skin.'

Anne Applebaum, *Red Famine*, p.248.

Average life expectancies of children born in 1933:

Boys 5 years

Girls 8 years[2]

A young girl, victim of the famine, Kharkiv, 1933.[3]

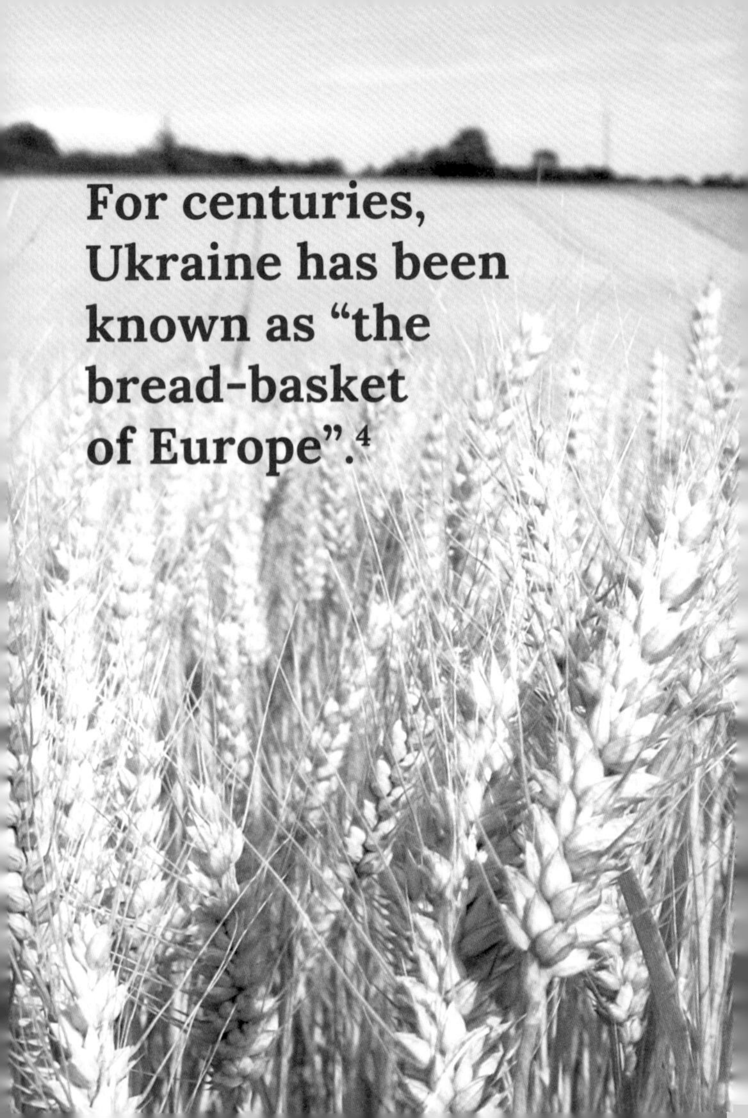

For centuries, Ukraine has been known as "the bread-basket of Europe".[4]

The 'black earth' of Ukraine is extremely fertile. The climate is mild.

It is easily possible to have two harvests a year.

Herodotus remarked on the fertility of the soil in the 5th Century BC.

In recent times, Ukraine exported 40-50 million tonnes of cereal a year, prior to 2022.[5]

Ukraine is not a place where a famine should ever take place.

Causes of the famine:

1. Collectivisation.
2. Forcible seizures of grain and other food.

Soviet authorities taking food from peasants, Novokrasne, Mykolaiv Oblast [administrative region], November 1932.[6]

Collectivisation

Collectivisation began gradually under Lenin's 'co-operative plan' in 1921.[7] Peasants and farmers gave up their individually-owned farms and joined large collective farms.

In 1929, Stalin launched a big new collectivisation campaign. Peasants were forced to join collective farms and in much greater numbers.

By 10 March 1930, 65% of farms and 70% of working animals had been collectivised.[8]

Farmers big and small no longer owned their own property, so did not have a strong incentive to make sure the farms were productive. Output fell.

Exports of grain from the Soviet Union fell dramatically from what they had been before the communist revolution and the enforced collectivisation.

1913 **9 million tons**

1930 **4.8 million tons**

1932 **1.7 million tons**[9]

Ukraine's autumn harvest in 1932 was 60% lower than central planners had expected it to be.[10]

At this point, it was clear that famine was coming.

Children digging up potatoes in frozen conditions on a collective farm, Donetsk Oblast [administrative region], 1933.[11]

Seizures of grain and other food.

Although the harvest was lower, Stalin insisted on large quotas of grain being exported from Ukraine. He wanted the grain to feed the cities and to export to raise foreign currency.

The grain quota Stalin imposed in 1930 and 1931 was 115% above the 1926-27 quota, although collectivisation had decreased the yield.[12]

Communist cadres confiscating grain from peasants, Novokrasne, Mykolaiv Oblast [region], Ukraine, 1932.[13]

Peasants became desperate to survive.

Secret police documented peasants hiding grain in "pits" and hidden storage sites dotted around villages.[14]

Communist cadres from the towns conducted house-to-house searches. They used long rods with metal hooks on the end to probe for food in every corner of each house. They dug up the earth around houses and broke through walls.

They confiscated everything edible.[15]

Mikhail Sholokhov, a famous Russian writer and Stalin supporter, wrote to him listing 16 ways in which 593 tonnes of bread were extracted from farmers. These are three of them:

> *1. Mass beatings of collective farmers and individual farmers....*
>
> *3. In the Vaschaev collective farm, collective farmers were doused with kerosene on the legs and hem of their skirts, lit, and then extinguished: "Tell me where the pit is! I'll set it on fire again!" On the same collective farm, the person being interrogated was put in a pit, buried halfway and the interrogation continued....*
>
> *6. In the Lebyazhensky collective farm they were put against the wall and shots were fired past the heads of the interrogated from shotguns.*[16]

1931 The seizures left each peasant with an average of 112 kg of grain, equivalent to just over 1,000 calories a day for the winter and the following spring.

1932 Less grain could be extracted by the state after a reduced harvest but the seizures were so brutal and determined that they left the peasants with an average of only 83 kg of grain, equivalent to about 750 calories a day.[17]

The average man needs 2500 calories a day and the average woman 2000.[18]

Interview with a Ukrainian woman who escaped to Canada, 13th September, 1933.

Q: *What is the reason for the famine? Has there been a drought or a bad harvest, or are you not sowing anything?*

A: *There has been a harvest, we sow and we plant, but as soon as anything grows, they take it all away and pack it off to Moscow. We had a good harvest this summer, but so what? They sent in the machines, cut everything, threshed it, and left not a kernel behind. They took everything. People were weeping. They asked "What will we eat?" But the Chekists [secret policemen] laughed and answered: "You'll find something." What will people not do in order to hide some grain for themselves! They hide it in their hair, they hide it in their mouth, beneath their tongue, but they search it out and take it too.*

Q: *And how do people live in Moscow? In the Moscow region? Is there a famine there?*

A: No, *there is no famine there. There is enough of everything. When I arrived in Moscow, I could buy everything I wanted at the bazaar – bread and meat and vegetables.*

Interview in *The Ukrainian Voice*, Winnipeg, 13 September 1933.[19]

Stalin knew about the famine

Letter to Stalin, 10 June 1932.

I was in many villages and saw a considerable part of the countryside engulfed in famine... They are eating food scraps from the bottom of the barrel, if any are available.

Grigory Petrovsky,
President of the Executive Committee of Ukrainian Soviets.[20]

Letter to Stalin, 10 June 1932.

In March and April, there were tens of thousands of malnourished, starving and swollen people dying from famine in every village; children abandoned by their parents and orphans appeared.

Vlas Chubar,
Chairman of the Council of People's Commissars
of the Ukrainian Soviet Socialist Republic.[21]

Letter to Stalin, 4 April 1933.

In this region, as in other regions, collective farmers and individual farmers are now dying of starvation; adults and children swell up and eat everything that a person is not supposed to eat, starting with carrion and ending with oak bark and all kinds of swamp roots.

Mikhail Sholokhov,
supporter of Stalin.

Although Stalin was told about the famine he did not publicly acknowledge it and he continued to demand millions of tonnes of grain, thus ensuring a terrible famine.

He claimed to doubt the information he was given, even though it had come from communist leaders on the spot.

> *I did not like the letters from Chubar and Petrovsky. The former spouts 'self-criticism' in order to secure a million more poods of bread from Moscow, the latter is feigning sainthood, claiming victimisation from the [Central Committee] in order to reduce grain procurement levels... In my opinion, Ukraine has been given more than enough...*
>
> Stalin, letter to Kaganovich,
> Second Secretary of the Communist Party
> of the Soviet Union, 10 June, 1932.

Instead, Stalin blamed Ukrainians themselves and made their conditions even worse.

7 August 1932: Stalin passed a decree which became known among the peasants as 'The Law on Five Ears of Grain'.

Any peasant taking grain from collective farms for their own use was to be punished with execution or ten years' imprisonment.

Within 6 months, 100,000 Ukrainians had been sent to hard labour camps and 4,500 had been executed for taking even a few ears of grain or leftover crops from collective farms.[22]

31 December 1932: a special passport system was introduced preventing peasants from living or working in cities, where factory workers were still allowed a small amount of pay and food.

Nevertheless, thousands attempted to migrate from rural areas to towns to beg for food.

Hungry peasants leaving the countryside to find food in the cities, 1933.[23]

In 1933, people were dying of starvation in the street, even in Kyiv, the capital of Ukraine. Their bodies had to be collected:

January:	**400 corpses**
February:	**518 corpses**
The first eight days of March:	**248 corpses**[24]

Victims of the famine, Kharkiv, 1933.[25]

In Kharkiv, 18,000 children of peasants were abandoned by their parents during the famine.

The parents knew they themselves would be caught by the secret police and sent back to the countryside. They thought their children had better chances of survival as orphan beggars in the city than in the countryside.[26]

20 November 1932: A 'blacklist system' penalised villages that failed to meet grain quotas.

Blacklisted villages had their grain supplies and livestock confiscated and they were blockaded by the secret police. 37 of the 392 districts in Ukraine were 'blacklisted' in this way.[27]

January 1933: Stalin closed the borders of Ukraine with armed guards, effectively trapping Ukrainians within the famine zone to be starved to death.

Victims of the famine in the street, Kharkiv, 1933.[28]

Stalin convened a joint plenum of the Central Committee and Central Control Commission of the Communist Party from September 28th to October 2nd 1933 in Moscow.

The plenum attendees were supplied with several tons of meat, sausage, chicken and fish, 300 kilos of caviar, 600 kilos of cheeses and large amounts of fruit, mushrooms and other vegetables. The attendees were allowed to take home some of the surplus.[29]

What were Stalin's motives for making the famine worse?

Historians disagree. He certainly wanted food for Russian cities and for export to gain foreign exchange. But Ukraine may have been singled out for particularly cruel treatment because it had been, for a long time, resistant to Soviet authority.

Between 1917 and 1921, the Ukrainian War of Independence took place. There was a complex struggle for power. Six different armies operated on its territory. Kyiv changed hands five times in less than a year. For a while, a Ukrainian monarch known as the Hetman was in power.[30] Symon Petliura led a separate nationalist army.

Eventually those fighting for independence were defeated by Soviet forces. But nationalism was never far below the surface as the Soviet secret police reported. Resistance to Stalin's compulsory collectivisation of farms was at its most forceful in Ukraine.

Stalin may have thought that famine and his harsh measures would crush resistance for years to come.

Stalin was even worried about the loyalty of members of the Ukrainian Communist Party.

> *"The Ukrainian Communist party... contains quite a few (yes, many!) rotten elements and unconscious Petliurites.... Without these and similar measures [of repression]...we may lose Ukraine."*
>
> Stalin letter, 11th August 1932.[31]

The Terror-Famine of 1932-33 was a dual-purpose by-product of collectivisation, designed to suppress Ukrainian nationalism and the most important concentration of prosperous peasants at one throw.

Norman Davies,
Europe: A History.[32]

...more aggressive purchases of food abroad and open appeals for international assistance **could have averted many (and perhaps most) of the deaths. The world had plenty of food in 1933** *– indeed, the glut was depressing global prices for grain - but Stalin refused to reveal vulnerability, which, in his mind, would incite enemies. Admission also would have been a global propaganda debacle, undermining the boasts about the Five-Year Plan and the collective farms.*

Professor Stephen Kotkin,
Stalin – Waiting for Hitler 1929-41.[33]

Stalin refused to acknowledge the famine.

It was prohibited to record the real number of deaths. It was forbidden to record the cause of death as “hunger”. Instead, death certificates had to list “old age”, “typhus” or “exhaustion”.[34]

The census bureau made an estimate that the 1934 population of the Soviet Union, including Ukraine, was 168 million. A proper census was to be published in 1937. The government was looking for an increase to 170 or even 172 million. But the census revealed that **the population had fallen to 162 million due to famine deaths** and the babies not born who otherwise would have been alive.[35]

The truth was unacceptable to Stalin.

The figures were not published. The head of the census bureau, Ivan Kraval, was arrested and executed.[36]

The Soviet authorities denied to western journalists that a famine was taking place.

Walter Duranty, the Moscow correspondent of the *New York Times*, in one of the most shameful moments in the history of western journalism, repeated this lie. He wrote in his newspaper on 31 March 1933: "There is no actual starvation or deaths from starvation, but there is widespread mortality from diseases due to malnutrition."[37]

However, a British journalist, Gareth Jones, travelled to Ukraine in March 1933 to see for himself. He was horrified by what he discovered.[38]

Everywhere was the cry, 'There is no bread. We are dying. This cry came from every part of Russia, from the Volga, Siberia, White Russia, the North Caucasus, Central Asia. I tramped through the black earth region [Ukraine] because that was once the richest farmland in Russia and because the correspondents have been forbidden to go there to see for themselves what is happening.

Gareth Jones, Berlin Press Conference,
19 March, 1933.[39]

In the train a Communist denied to me that there was a famine. I flung a crust of bread which I had been eating from my own supply into a spittoon. A peasant fellow-passenger fished it out and ravenously ate it. I threw an orange peel into the spittoon and the peasant again grabbed it and devoured it. The Communist subsided. I stayed overnight in a village where there used to be 200 oxen and where there now are six. The peasants were eating the cattle fodder and had only a month's supply left.

They told me that many had already died of hunger. Two soldiers came to arrest a thief. They warned me against travel by night as there were too many 'starving' desperate men.

Gareth Jones, Berlin Press Conference, 19 March, 1933.[40]

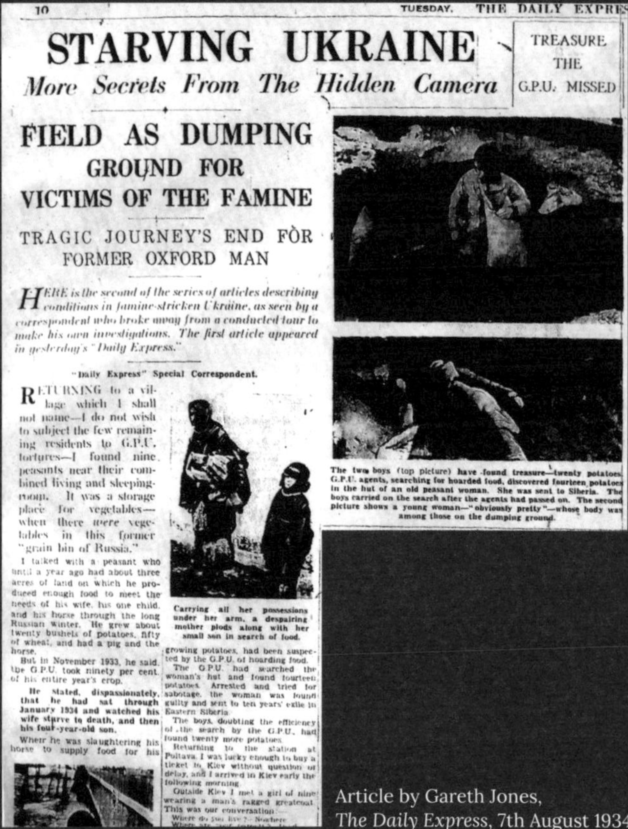

10 TUESDAY. THE DAILY EXPRES[S]

STARVING UKRAINE

More Secrets From The Hidden Camera

TREASURE THE G.P.U. MISSED

FIELD AS DUMPING GROUND FOR VICTIMS OF THE FAMINE

TRAGIC JOURNEY'S END FOR FORMER OXFORD MAN

HERE is the second of the series of articles describing conditions in famine-stricken Ukraine, as seen by a correspondent who broke away from a conducted tour to make his own investigations. The first article appeared in yesterday's "Daily Express."

"Daily Express" Special Correspondent.

RETURNING to a village which I shall not name—I do not wish to subject the few remaining residents to G.P.U. tortures—I found nine peasants near their combined living and sleeping-room. It was a storage place for vegetables—when there *were* vegetables in this former "grain bin of Russia."

I talked with a peasant who until a year ago had about three acres of land on which he produced enough food to meet the needs of his wife, his one child, and his horse through the long Russian winter. He grew about twenty bushels of potatoes, fifty of wheat, and had a pig and the horse.

But in November 1933, he said, the G.P.U. took ninety per cent. of his entire year's crop.

He stated, dispassionately, that he had sat through January 1934 and watched his wife starve to death, and then his four-year-old son.

When he was slaughtering his horse to supply food for his

Carrying all her possessions under her arm, a despairing mother plods along with her small son in search of food.

growing potatoes, had been suspected by the G.P.U. of hoarding food.

The G.P.U. had searched the woman's hut and found fourteen potatoes. Arrested and tried for sabotage, the woman was found guilty and sent to ten years' exile in Eastern Siberia.

The boys, doubting the efficiency of the search by the G.P.U., had found twenty more potatoes.

Returning to the station at Poltava, I was lucky enough to buy a ticket to Kiev without question or delay, and I arrived in Kiev early the following morning.

Outside Kiev I met a girl of nine wearing a man's ragged greatcoat. This was our conversation:—

Where do you live?—Nowhere.

The two boys (top picture) have found treasure—twenty potatoes. G.P.U. agents, searching for hoarded food, discovered fourteen potatoes in the hut of an old peasant woman. She was sent to Siberia. The boys carried on the search after the agents had passed on. The second picture shows a young woman—"obviously pretty"—whose body was among those on the dumping ground.

Article by Gareth Jones,
The Daily Express, 7th August 1934

Mr Jones is a semi-fictionalised film made about Gareth Jones and his reporting of the Holodomor.

For 50 years, the Soviet Union tried to hide the famine and deny its existence.

Reports were censored and archives destroyed. Ukrainians would have been putting their lives in danger if they talked about it.

It has taken many years since the collapse of the Soviet Union in 1991 for the Holodomor to receive the international recognition it deserves.

Estimates of the deaths from the Holodomor have ranged between 3.5 million and 10 million. The figure of 3.9 million cited in this booklet is based on research sponsored by the Institute of Demography and Social Research of the Ukrainian National Academy of Sciences and the Harvard Ukrainian Research Institute. This figure is also cited by Anne Applebaum in her book on the subject, *Red Famine.*[41]

The population of Ukraine at this time was about 33 million.[42] So **more than 10 per cent of the population perished.**

Ukraine was simultaneously the most fertile part of the Soviet Union and suffered the worst famine. But other areas suffered too, most notably the Kazakh autonomous republic where between 1.2 and 1.4 million died.[43]

The Holodomor is commemorated every year on the fourth Saturday of November.

There are services in Ukrainian churches across the UK and in other parts of the world. Some people also light candles and put them in their front windows at dusk.

Rishi Sunak, the United Kingdom Prime Minister, lit a candle in Kyiv to honour the victims of the Holodomor, accompanied by President Zelensky, in November 2022.[44]

The Holodomor memorial in Kyiv.[45]

This is not simply a case of mass murder. It is a case of genocide, of destruction, not of individuals only, but of a culture and a nation.

Raphael Lemkin

Raphael Lemkin was a Polish lawyer who coined the term "genocide". He made this remark at the 20th Commemoration of the Holodomor, New York City, 1953.[46]

Endnotes:

1 HREC, 'Resources: Global Holodomor Recognition'. [accessed 20/07/2023] https://holodomor.ca/resources/memorialization/global-holodomor-recognition/

2 Anne Applebaum, *Red Famine: Stalin's War on Ukraine* (London: Penguin Books, 2017), 285.

3 Image credit: Alexander Wienerberger.

4 Image credit: public domain.

5 OECD, 'The impacts and policy implications of Russia's aggression against Ukraine on agricultural markets', 5 August 2022. https://www.oecd.org/ukraine-hub/policy-responses/the-impacts-and-policy-implications-of-russia-s-aggression-against-ukraine-on-agricultural-markets-0030a4cd/and John Reed et al, 'How Russia's war in Ukraine upended the breadbasket of Europe', *Financial Times*, 27 April 2022. https://ig.ft.com/ukraine-war-food-insecurity/

6 Image credit: Public domain.

7 Vsevolod Holubnychy, 'Collectivisation', *Encyclopaedia of Ukraine*, vol. 1 (1984), accessed through the *Internet Encyclopaedia of Ukraine*. https://www.encyclopediaofukraine.com/display.asp?linkpath=pages%5CC%5CO%5CCollectivization.htm#:~:text=Vladimir%20Lenin's%20'co%2D,to%20work%20their%20land%20jointly

8 Ibid. Image credit: Wikimedia Commons.

9 Stephen Kotkin, *Stalin, Waiting for Hitler* 1929-41 (Allen Lane, 2017) 107.

10 Anne Applebaum, *Red Famine: Stalin's War on Ukraine* (London: Penguin Books, 2017), 193.

11 Image credit: Wikimedia Commons (cropped)

12 Vsevolod Holubnychy, 'Collectivisation', *Encyclopaedia of Ukraine*, vol. 1 (1984), accessed through the *Internet Encyclopaedia of Ukraine*. https://www.encyclopediaofukraine.com/display.asp?linkpath=pages%5CC%5CO%5CCollectivization.htm#:~:text=Vladimir%20Lenin's%20'co%2D,to%20work%20their%20land%20jointly

13 Image credit: history.org.ua (creative commons)

14 Nicolas Werth, *The Great Ukrainian Famine of* 1932-33, *Mass Violence & Resistance*, [online], 18 April 2008, https://www.sciencespo.fr/mass-violence-war-massacre-resistance/en/document/great-ukrainian-famine-1932-33.html

15 Anne Applebaum, *Red Famine: Stalin's War on Ukraine* (London:

Penguin Books, 2017), 227. And University of Minnesota College of Liberal Arts, 'Holodomor and Genocide Studies', https://cla.umn.edu/chgs/holocaust-genocide-education/resource-guides/holodomor

16 V. Danilov, R. Manning, L. Viola, eds., *The Tragedy of the Russian Village. Collectivisation and Dekulakisation. Documents and Materials. Volume 3. End of 1930-33.* (Moscow: ROSSPEN, 2000), 717-720.

17 Vsevolod Holubnychy, 'Collectivisation', *Encyclopaedia of Ukraine*, vol. 1 (1984), accessed through the *Internet Encyclopaedia of Ukraine*. https://www.encyclopediaofukraine.com/display.asp?linkpath=pages%5CC%5CO%5CCollectivization.htm#:~:text=Vladimir%20Lenin's%20'co%2D,to%20work%20their%20land%20jointly

18 British Heart Foundation, 'Heart Matters'. [accessed 27/07/2023] https://www.bhf.org.uk/informationsupport/heart-matters-magazine/nutrition/how-many-calories-should-i-eat-a-day

19 Bohdan Klid and Alexander J. Motyl, *Holodomor Reader: A Sourcebook on the Famine of 1932-1933 in Ukraine.* (Toronto: CIUS Press, 2012.). Page 2 of "Survivor testimonies, memoirs, diaries, and letters" [accessed 10 August 2023] https://holodomor.ca/resource/holodomor-reader-a-sourcebook-on-the-famine-of-1932-1933-in-ukraine/

20 Anne Applebaum, *Red Famine: Stalin's War on Ukraine* (London: Penguin Books, 2017), 179. Image credit: public domain.

21 Anne Applebaum, *Red Famine: Stalin's War on Ukraine* (London: Penguin Books, 2017), 180. Image credit: public domain.

22 Ibid, 186.

23 Image credit: Alexander Wienerberger, near Kharkiv, 1933.

24 Anne Applebaum, *Red Famine: Stalin's War on Ukraine* (London: Penguin Books, 2017), 204.

25 Image credit: Alexander Wienerberger.

26 National Museum of the Holodomor-Genocide, *Raphael Lemkin: Soviet Genocide in Ukraine* (Kyiv: Marko Melnyk Publishing House, 2020), 50.

27 Harvard Ukrainian Research Institute, 'The Great Famine Project: Blacklisted Localities', https://gis.huri.harvard.edu/blacklisted-localities

28 Image credit: Alexander Wienerberger.

29 *Stalin – Waiting for Hitler* 1929-41 by Stephen Kotkin, p 107.

30 Anne Applebaum, *Red Famine: Stalin's War on Ukraine* (London: Penguin Books, 2017), 16-17.

31 Letter to Kaganovich cited in *Stalin – Waiting for Hitler* by Stephen Kotkin, p102.
32 Norman Davies, *Europe: A History*, (Oxford: Oxford University Press, 1998).
33 Page 129.
34 Holodomor Museum, 'Holodomor History', [accessed 05/07/2023] https://holodomormuseum.org.ua/en/the-history-of-the-holodomor/
35 Anne Applebaum, *Red Famine: Stalin's War on Ukraine* (London: Penguin Books, 2017), 306-7.
36 Time Note, 'Ivan Kraval', [accessed 10/08/2023]. https://timenote.info/en/Ivan-Kraval. Image credit: http://www.sakharov-center.ru/
37 garethjones.org, 'The denigration of Gareth Jones by Walter Duranty in *The New York Times*, Friday March 31st 1933.' [accessed 19/07/2023] https://www.garethjones.org/soviet_articles/russians_hungry_not_starving.htm
38 garethjones.org, 'The Western Mail, April 11th, 1931.' [accessed 19/07/2023] https://www.garethjones.org/soviet_articles/mixture_of_successes.htm. Image credit: public domain.
39 garethjones.org, 'Famine Exposure Newspaper Articles relating to Gareth Jones' trips to The Soviet Union (1930-35)' [accessed 19/07/2023] https://www.garethjones.org/soviet_articles/soviet_articles.htm
40 Ibid.
41 Anne Applebaum, *Red Famine: Stalin's War on Ukraine* (London: Penguin Books, 2017), 284. See also: Harvard Ukrainian Research Institute, 'The Great Famine Project', https://gis.huri.harvard.edu/demography-man-made-human-catastrophe
42 *Stalin – Waiting for Hitler* 1929-41 by Stephen Kotkin, p127.
43 Ditto.
44 Image credit: Ukrinform TV. See https://www.youtube.com/watch?v=laRnkKf9eEI&t=183s
45 Image credit: Steve Haslam, 2012.
46 HREC Education, 'Role of Lemkin', [accessed 10/08/2023] https://education.holodomor.ca/teaching-materials/role-of-lemkin/
47 Metropolitan Epiphanius, primate of the Orthodox Church of Ukraine, November 2019. https://www.rferl.org/a/ukrainians-mourn-millions-of-stalin-era-famine-s-victims/30288132.html